W D W
Magical Trip Planner

Suitable for planning
Vacations to Walt Disney World
Orlando Florida

Our WDW Magical Trip Planner – Suitable for planning vacations to Walt Disney World Orlando Florida is the perfect planning guide for your upcoming Disney Trip.

With years of experience holidaying at Disney and the surrounding areas of Orlando we know that planning your perfect trip to see the mouse can be a minefield.

There's heaps to plan from arranging your travel and sorting your ESTA to setting countdowns in your calendar for important booking windows such as Dining ADRs and Fast Passes.

With our planner you can keep all your plans, bookings, and daily park schedules in one travel sized book to take with you each day to the parks as it fits nicely in your backpack.

We also have budget sheets, ADR dining costings, snack list and packing and shopping lists. We've got you covered helping to make your Disney vacation planning a breeze.

Write up daily trip review memoirs and keep all your magical memories to look

back on for your next trip. Please help other holiday makers find us by leaving

feedback at the site you purchased the book from.

And finally we hope you have a magical trip to see the MOUSE!

First Publication May 2020
Second Publication Nov 2021

© 2020 Magical Planner Co.

Trip Details

Date	
Party	

Rough Plans

Planning Timeline – To do

12 MONTHS +

6 MONTHS

3 MONTHS

1 MONTH

3 WEEKS

2 WEEKS

1 WEEK

1-2 DAYS

Notes

_____
_____
_____
_____
_____
_____
_____
_____
_____
_____
_____
_____
_____
_____
_____
_____
_____
_____
_____
_____
_____

Notes

_____
_____
_____
_____
_____
_____
_____
_____
_____
_____
_____
_____
_____
_____
_____
_____
_____
_____
_____
_____
_____
_____

Holiday Planning Comparisons

PACKAGE NAME: _____ **ONSITE ☐ / OFFSITE ☐**

Dates: /   /   TO   /   /

Resort:

Ticket Package Included:

Dining Plan Included:

Notes:

Room Type:

Promo cards:

Parking Costs:

Estimated Spends:

TOTAL COST

PACKAGE NAME: _____ **ONSITE ☐ / OFFSITE ☐**

Dates: /   /   TO   /   /

Resort:

Ticket Package Included:

Dining Plan Included:

Notes:

Room Type:

Promo cards:

Parking Costs:

Estimated Spends:

TOTAL COST

PACKAGE NAME: _____ **ONSITE ☐ / OFFSITE ☐**

Dates: /   /   TO   /   /

Resort:

Ticket Package Included:

Dining Plan Included:

Notes:

Room Type:

Promo cards:

Parking Costs:

Estimated Spends:

TOTAL COST

Holiday Planning Comparisons

PACKAGE NAME: _____ **ONSITE ☐ / OFFSITE ☐**

Dates: /   /   TO   /   /

Resort:

Ticket Package Included:

Dining Plan Included:

Notes:

Room Type:

Promo cards:

Parking Costs:

Estimated Spends:

TOTAL COST

_____

PACKAGE NAME: _____ **ONSITE ☐ / OFFSITE ☐**

Dates: /   /   TO   /   /

Resort:

Ticket Package Included:

Dining Plan Included:

Notes:

Room Type:

Promo cards:

Parking Costs:

Estimated Spends:

TOTAL COST

_____

PACKAGE NAME: _____ **ONSITE ☐ / OFFSITE ☐**

Dates: /   /   TO   /   /

Resort:

Ticket Package Included:

Dining Plan Included:

Notes:

Room Type:

Promo cards:

Parking Costs:

Estimated Spends:

TOTAL COST

_____

Travel Details

✈ Air Travel:	Date:
FLIGHT No.	AIRLINE:
DEPAR ⊙	🕐
ARRIVE: ⊙	🕐

✈ Air Travel:	Date:
FLIGHT No.	AIRLINE:
DEPAR ⊙	🕐
ARRIVE: ⊙	🕐

🚗 Car Hire Company:	Date:
BOOKING No.	CAR GROUP:
PICK UP: ⊙	🕐
RETURN: ⊙	🕐

🚗 Transport to Resort:	Date:
CONFIRMATION No.	LOCATION:
DEPAR ⊙	🕐
ARRIVE: ⊙	🕐

Visas & Estas Done ☐

Travel Details

✈ Air Travel:	Date:
FLIGHT No.	AIRLINE:
DEPAR : 📍	🕐
ARRIVE: 📍	🕐

✈ Air Travel:	Date:
FLIGHT No.	AIRLINE:
DEPAR : 📍	🕐
ARRIVE: 📍	🕐

🚕 Car Hire Company:	Date:
BOOKING No.	CAR GROUP:
PICK UP: 📍	🕐
RETURN: 📍	🕐

🚕 Transport to Resort:	Date:
CONFIRMATION No.	LOCATION:
DEPAR : 📍	🕐
ARRIVE: 📍	🕐

Visas & Estas Done ☐

Accommodation Details

Resort Name:	Booking No:

CHECK IN: CHECK OUT:

ADDRESS:

ONSITE DINING:

RECREATION:

SPECIAL REQUESTS / ROOM LOCATION:

Resort Name:	Booking No:

CHECK IN: CHECK OUT:

ADDRESS:

ONSITE DINING:

RECREATION:

SPECIAL REQUESTS / ROOM LOCATION:

Accommodation Details

Resort Name:	Booking No:

CHECK IN: CHECK OUT:

ADDRESS:

ONSITE DINING:

RECREATION:

SPECIAL REQUESTS / ROOM LOCATION:

Resort Name:	Booking No:

CHECK IN: CHECK OUT:

ADDRESS:

ONSITE DINING:

RECREATION:

SPECIAL REQUESTS / ROOM LOCATION:

Budget And Payment Tracker

Vacation Budget $ £

Date	Item	Amount	Due	Balance

Budget And Payment Tracker

Vacation Budget $ £

Date	Item	Amount	Due	Balance

Mouse Saving Chart

Total Saving Goal

= $

100 Day Countdown

Trip Date: / /

Days Till We're Off To Disney World

100	99	98	97	96	95	94	93	92	90
89	88	87	86	85	84	83	82	81	80
79	78	77	76	75	74	73	72	71	70
69	68	67	66	65	64	63	62	61	60
59	58	57	56	55	54	53	52	51	50
49	48	47	46	45	44	43	42	41	40
39	38	37	36	35	34	33	32	31	30
29	28	27	26	25	24	23	22	21	20
19	18	17	16	15	14	13	12	11	10
9	8	7	6			3	2	1	

Packing List

☐ _____   ☐ _____
☐ _____   ☐ _____
☐ _____   ☐ _____
☐ _____   ☐ _____
☐ _____   ☐ _____
☐ _____   ☐ _____
☐ _____   ☐ _____
☐ _____   ☐ _____
☐ _____   ☐ _____
☐ _____   ☐ _____
☐ _____   ☐ _____
☐ _____   ☐ _____
☐ _____   ☐ _____
☐ _____   ☐ _____
☐ _____   ☐ _____
☐ _____   ☐ _____
☐ _____   ☐ _____
☐ _____   ☐ _____
☐ _____   ☐ _____
☐ _____   ☐ _____
☐ _____   ☐ _____
☐ _____   ☐ _____
☐ _____   ☐ _____
☐ _____   ☐ _____

Family Packing List

NAME: _____ ITEM   NAME: _____ ITEM

☐ _____   ☐ _____
☐ _____   ☐ _____
☐ _____   ☐ _____
☐ _____   ☐ _____
☐ _____   ☐ _____
☐ _____   ☐ _____
☐ _____   ☐ _____
☐ _____   ☐ _____
☐ _____   ☐ _____
☐ _____   ☐ _____
☐ _____   ☐ _____
☐ _____   ☐ _____
☐ _____   ☐ _____
☐ _____   ☐ _____
☐ _____   ☐ _____
☐ _____   ☐ _____
☐ _____   ☐ _____
☐ _____   ☐ _____
☐ _____   ☐ _____
☐ _____   ☐ _____
☐ _____   ☐ _____
☐ _____   ☐ _____
☐ _____   ☐ _____
☐ _____   ☐ _____
☐ _____   ☐ _____
☐ _____   ☐ _____
☐ _____   ☐ _____

Family Packing List

NAME: _____ ITEM

- [ ] _____
- [ ] _____
- [ ] _____
- [ ] _____
- [ ] _____
- [ ] _____
- [ ] _____
- [ ] _____
- [ ] _____
- [ ] _____
- [ ] _____
- [ ] _____
- [ ] _____
- [ ] _____
- [ ] _____
- [ ] _____
- [ ] _____
- [ ] _____
- [ ] _____
- [ ] _____
- [ ] _____
- [ ] _____
- [ ] _____
- [ ] _____
- [ ] _____

NAME: _____ ITEM

- [ ] _____
- [ ] _____
- [ ] _____
- [ ] _____
- [ ] _____
- [ ] _____
- [ ] _____
- [ ] _____
- [ ] _____
- [ ] _____
- [ ] _____
- [ ] _____
- [ ] _____
- [ ] _____
- [ ] _____
- [ ] _____
- [ ] _____
- [ ] _____
- [ ] _____
- [ ] _____
- [ ] _____
- [ ] _____
- [ ] _____
- [ ] _____
- [ ] _____

Things to Buy

BEFORE   ITEM   ITEM

☐ _____ ☐ _____
☐ _____ ☐ _____
☐ _____ ☐ _____
☐ _____ ☐ _____
☐ _____ ☐ _____
☐ _____ ☐ _____
☐ _____ ☐ _____
☐ _____ ☐ _____
☐ _____ ☐ _____
☐ _____ ☐ _____
☐ _____ ☐ _____
☐ _____ ☐ _____

ON ARRIVAL   ITEM   ITEM

☐ _____ ☐ _____
☐ _____ ☐ _____
☐ _____ ☐ _____
☐ _____ ☐ _____
☐ _____ ☐ _____
☐ _____ ☐ _____
☐ _____ ☐ _____
☐ _____ ☐ _____
☐ _____ ☐ _____
☐ _____ ☐ _____
☐ _____ ☐ _____
☐ _____ ☐ _____

15 Day Basic Plan

DATE	DATE	DATE	DATE	DATE
AM	AM	AM	AM	AM
PM	PM	PM	PM	PM

DATE	DATE	DATE	DATE	DATE
AM	**AM**	AM	AM	AM
PM	**PM**	PM	PM	PM

DATE	DATE	DATE	DATE	DATE
AM	AM	AM	AM	AM
PM	PM	PM	PM	PM

Don't forget you'll need to use the Disney app to make your advanced park day reservations at present.

15 Day Basic Plan

DATE	DATE	DATE	DATE	DATE
AM	AM	AM	AM	AM
PM	PM	PM	PM	PM

DATE	DATE	DATE	DATE	DATE
AM	**AM**	AM	AM	AM
PM	**PM**	PM	PM	PM

DATE	DATE	DATE	DATE	DATE
AM	AM	AM	AM	AM
PM	PM	PM	PM	PM

15 Day Basic Plan vs2

DATE	DATE	DATE	DATE	DATE
AM	AM	AM	AM	AM
PM	PM	PM	PM	PM

DATE	DATE	DATE	DATE	DATE
AM	**AM**	AM	AM	AM
PM	**PM**	PM	PM	PM

DATE	DATE	DATE	DATE	DATE
AM	AM	AM	AM	AM
PM	PM	PM	PM	PM

Don't forget you'll need to use the Disney app to make your advanced park day reservations at present.

15 Day Basic Plan vs2

DATE	DATE	DATE	DATE	DATE
AM	AM	AM	AM	AM
PM	PM	PM	PM	PM

DATE	DATE	DATE	DATE	DATE
AM	**AM**	AM	AM	AM
PM	**PM**	PM	PM	PM

DATE	DATE	DATE	DATE	DATE
AM	AM	AM	AM	AM
PM	PM	PM	PM	PM

Dining Planning

Snacks To Try

ITEM	LOCATION	CREDIT / COST $
		☐ /$
		☐ /$
		☐ /$
		☐ /$
		☐ /$
		☐ /$
		☐ /$
		☐ /$
		☐ /$
		☐ /$
		☐ /$
		☐ /$
		☐ /$
		☐ /$
		☐ /$
		☐ /$
		☐ /$
		☐ /$
		☐ /$
		☐ /$
		☐ /$

Dining Planning

Snacks To Try

ITEM	LOCATION	CREDIT / COST $
		☐ /$
		☐ /$
		☐ /$
		☐ /$
		☐ /$
		☐ /$
		☐ /$
		☐ /$
		☐ /$
		☐ /$
		☐ /$
		☐ /$
		☐ /$
		☐ /$
		☐ /$
		☐ /$
		☐ /$
		☐ /$
		☐ /$
		☐ /$
		☐ /$
		☐ /$

Dining Planning

Quick Service Dining

NAME	LOCATION	CREDIT / COST $	
		☐	/$
		☐	/$
		☐	/$
		☐	/$
		☐	/$
		☐	/$
		☐	/$
		☐	/$
		☐	/$
		☐	/$
		☐	/$
		☐	/$
		☐	/$
		☐	/$
		☐	/$
		☐	/$
		☐	/$
		☐	/$
		☐	/$
		☐	/$
		☐	/$

Dining Planning

Quick Service Dining

NAME	LOCATION	CREDIT / COST $
		☐ /$
		☐ /$
		☐ /$
		☐ /$
		☐ /$
		☐ /$
		☐ /$
		☐ /$
		☐ /$
		☐ /$
		☐ /$
		☐ /$
		☐ /$
		☐ /$
		☐ /$
		☐ /$
		☐ /$
		☐ /$
		☐ /$
		☐ /$
		☐ /$

Dining Planning

Quick Service Dining

NAME	LOCATION	CREDIT / COST $
		☐ /$
		☐ /$
		☐ /$
		☐ /$
		☐ /$
		☐ /$
		☐ /$
		☐ /$
		☐ /$
		☐ /$
		☐ /$
		☐ /$
		☐ /$
		☐ /$
		☐ /$
		☐ /$
		☐ /$
		☐ /$
		☐ /$
		☐ /$
		☐ /$

Dining Planning

Quick Service Dining

NAME	LOCATION	CREDIT / COST $	
		☐	/$
		☐	/$
		☐	/$
		☐	/$
		☐	/$
		☐	/$
		☐	/$
		☐	/$
		☐	/$
		☐	/$
		☐	/$
		☐	/$
		☐	/$
		☐	/$
		☐	/$
		☐	/$
		☐	/$
		☐	/$
		☐	/$
		☐	/$
		☐	/$

ADR Dining Bookings
& Budgeting – 180 Days Prior to Check-In

Date: **Restaurant Name:**

BOOKING TIME: LOCATION: COVERS:

MEAL: B / L / D / S ESTIMATED MEAL COST TIP EST TOTAL

DDP CREDITS No: [ ] **+** **=**

NOTES:

Date: **Restaurant Name:**

BOOKING TIME: LOCATION: COVERS:

MEAL: B / L / D / S ESTIMATED MEAL COST TIP EST TOTAL

DDP CREDITS No: [ ] **+** **=**

NOTES:

Date: **Restaurant Name:**

BOOKING TIME: LOCATION: COVERS:

MEAL: B / L / D / S ESTIMATED MEAL COST TIP EST TOTAL

DDP CREDITS No: [ ] **+** **=**

NOTES:

Date: **Restaurant Name:**

BOOKING TIME: LOCATION: COVERS:

MEAL: B / L / D / S ESTIMATED MEAL COST TIP EST TOTAL

DDP CREDITS No: [ ] **+** **=**

NOTES:

ADR Dining Planning & Budgeting

Date: **Restaurant Name:**

BOOKING TIME: 🕐   LOCATION: 📍   COVERS:

MEAL: B / L / D / S   ESTIMATED MEAL COST   TIP   EST TOTAL

DDP CREDITS No: ☐   [   ]   **+**   [   ]   **=**   [   ]

NOTES:

_____

Date: **Restaurant Name:**

BOOKING TIME: 🕐   LOCATION: 📍   COVERS:

MEAL: B / L / D / S   ESTIMATED MEAL COST   TIP   EST TOTAL

DDP CREDITS No: ☐   [   ]   **+**   [   ]   **=**   [   ]

NOTES:

_____

Date: **Restaurant Name:**

BOOKING TIME: 🕐   LOCATION: 📍   COVERS:

MEAL: B / L / D / S   ESTIMATED MEAL COST   TIP   EST TOTAL

DDP CREDITS No: ☐   [   ]   **+**   [   ]   **=**   [   ]

NOTES:

_____

Date: **Restaurant Name:**

BOOKING TIME: 🕐   LOCATION: 📍   COVERS:

MEAL: B / L / D / S   ESTIMATED MEAL COST   TIP   EST TOTAL

DDP CREDITS No: ☐   [   ]   **+**   [   ]   **=**   [   ]

NOTES:

_____

ADR Dining Planning
& Budgeting

Date: **Restaurant Name:**

BOOKING TIME:

MEAL: B / L / D / S

DDP CREDITS No: ☐

NOTES:

LOCATION: COVERS:

ESTIMATED MEAL COST   TIP   EST TOTAL

☐ **+** ☐ **=** ☐

Date: **Restaurant Name:**

BOOKING TIME:

MEAL: B / L / D / S

DDP CREDITS No: ☐

NOTES:

LOCATION: COVERS:

ESTIMATED MEAL COST   TIP   EST TOTAL

☐ **+** ☐ **=** ☐

Date: **Restaurant Name:**

BOOKING TIME:

MEAL: B / L / D / S

DDP CREDITS No: ☐

NOTES:

LOCATION: COVERS:

ESTIMATED MEAL COST   TIP   EST TOTAL

☐ **+** ☐ **=** ☐

Date: **Restaurant Name:**

BOOKING TIME:

MEAL: B / L / D / S

DDP CREDITS No: ☐

NOTES:

LOCATION: COVERS:

ESTIMATED MEAL COST   TIP   EST TOTAL

☐ **+** ☐ **=** ☐

ADR Dining Planning
& Budgeting

| Restaurant Name:

BOOKING TIME: 🕐   LOCATION: 📍   COVERS:

MEAL: B / L / D / S   ESTIMATED MEAL COST   TIP   EST TOTAL

DDP CREDITS No: ☐   [   ] **+** [   ] **=** [   ]

NOTES:

_____

Date: | Restaurant Name:

BOOKING TIME: 🕐   LOCATION: 📍   COVERS:

MEAL: B / L / D / S   ESTIMATED MEAL COST   TIP   EST TOTAL

DDP CREDITS No: ☐   [   ] **+** [   ] **=** [   ]

NOTES:

_____

Date: | Restaurant Name:

BOOKING TIME: 🕐   LOCATION: 📍   COVERS:

MEAL: B / L / D / S   ESTIMATED MEAL COST   TIP   EST TOTAL

DDP CREDITS No: ☐   [   ] **+** [   ] **=** [   ]

NOTES:

_____

Date: | Restaurant Name:

BOOKING TIME: 🕐   LOCATION: 📍   COVERS:

MEAL: B / L / D / S   ESTIMATED MEAL COST   TIP   EST TOTAL

DDP CREDITS No: ☐   [   ] **+** [   ] **=** [   ]

NOTES:

_____

ADR Dining Planning
& Budgeting

Date: | **Restaurant Name:**

BOOKING TIME: ⬚   LOCATION: ⊙   COVERS:

MEAL: B / L / D / S   ESTIMATED MEAL COST   TIP   EST TOTAL

DDP CREDITS No: ⬚   ☐ **+** ☐ **=** ☐

NOTES:

Date: | **Restaurant Name:**

BOOKING TIME: ⬚   LOCATION: ⊙   COVERS:

MEAL: B / L / D / S   ESTIMATED MEAL COST   TIP   EST TOTAL

DDP CREDITS No: ⬚   ☐ **+** ☐ **=** ☐

NOTES:

Date: | **Restaurant Name:**

BOOKING TIME: ⬚   LOCATION: ⊙   COVERS:

MEAL: B / L / D / S   ESTIMATED MEAL COST   TIP   EST TOTAL

DDP CREDITS No: ⬚   ☐ **+** ☐ **=** ☐

NOTES:

Date: | **Restaurant Name:**

BOOKING TIME: ⬚   LOCATION: ⊙   COVERS:

MEAL: B / L / D / S   ESTIMATED MEAL COST   TIP   EST TOTAL

DDP CREDITS No: ⬚   ☐ **+** ☐ **=** ☐

NOTES:

ADR Dining Planning
& Budgeting

Date: **Restaurant Name:**

BOOKING TIME: LOCATION: COVERS:

MEAL: B / L / D / S   ESTIMATED MEAL COST   TIP   EST TOTAL

DDP CREDITS No: [   ] + [   ] = [   ]

NOTES:

Date: **Restaurant Name:**

BOOKING TIME: LOCATION: COVERS:

MEAL: B / L / D / S   ESTIMATED MEAL COST   TIP   EST TOTAL

DDP CREDITS No: [   ] + [   ] = [   ]

NOTES:

Date: **Restaurant Name:**

BOOKING TIME: LOCATION: COVERS:

MEAL: B / L / D / S   ESTIMATED MEAL COST   TIP   EST TOTAL

DDP CREDITS No: [   ] + [   ] = [   ]

NOTES:

Date: **Restaurant Name:**

BOOKING TIME: LOCATION: COVERS:

MEAL: B / L / D / S   ESTIMATED MEAL COST   TIP   EST TOTAL

DDP CREDITS No: [   ] + [   ] = [   ]

NOTES:

ADR Dining Planning
& Budgeting

Date: | **Restaurant Name:**

BOOKING TIME: | LOCATION: | COVERS:

MEAL: B / L / D / S | ESTIMATED MEAL COST | TIP | EST TOTAL

DDP CREDITS No: ☐ | [ ] **+** [ ] **=** [ ]

NOTES:

Date: | **Restaurant Name:**

BOOKING TIME: | LOCATION: | COVERS:

MEAL: B / L / D / S | ESTIMATED MEAL COST | TIP | EST TOTAL

DDP CREDITS No: ☐ | [ ] **+** [ ] **=** [ ]

NOTES:

Date: | **Restaurant Name:**

BOOKING TIME: | LOCATION: | COVERS:

MEAL: B / L / D / S | ESTIMATED MEAL COST | TIP | EST TOTAL

DDP CREDITS No: ☐ | [ ] **+** [ ] **=** [ ]

NOTES:

Date: | **Restaurant Name:**

BOOKING TIME: | LOCATION: | COVERS:

MEAL: B / L / D / S | ESTIMATED MEAL COST | TIP | EST TOTAL

DDP CREDITS No: ☐ | [ ] **+** [ ] **=** [ ]

NOTES:

ADR Dining Planning
Booking & Budgeting

BOOKING TIME: 🕐   LOCATION: 📍   COVERS:

MEAL: B / L / D / S   ESTIMATED MEAL COST   TIP   EST TOTAL

DDP CREDITS No: ☐   [   ] + [   ] = [   ]

NOTES:

BOOKING TIME: 🕐   LOCATION: 📍   COVERS:

MEAL: B / L / D / S   ESTIMATED MEAL COST   TIP   EST TOTAL

DDP CREDITS No: ☐   [   ] + [   ] = [   ]

NOTES:

BOOKING TIME: 🕐   LOCATION: 📍   COVERS:

MEAL: B / L / D / S   ESTIMATED MEAL COST   TIP   EST TOTAL

DDP CREDITS No: ☐   [   ] + [   ] = [   ]

NOTES:

BOOKING TIME: 🕐   LOCATION: 📍   COVERS:

MEAL: B / L / D / S   ESTIMATED MEAL COST   TIP   EST TOTAL

DDP CREDITS No: ☐   [   ] + [   ] = [   ]

NOTES:

Park Character Meet Wish List

Magic Kingdom Meet n Greets – Don't Forget Your Autograph Book
You can find further character dining in the appendix

Character Name	Park Location	Want to Meet ?
Magician Mickey	Town Square Theatre	
Tinker Bell	Town Square Theatre	
Cinderella	Princess Fairytale Hall	
Elena of Avalon	Princess Fairytale Hall	
Ariel	Ariel's Grotto	
Aladdin and Jasmine	Adventureland	
Mary Poppins	Liberty Square Gazebo	
Minnie, Daisy, Donald and Goofy	Pete's Silly Side Show	
Merida	Fairytale Garden	
Buzz Lightyear	Tomorrowland	
Jack Sparrow	Adventureland	
Peter Pan and Wendy	Adventureland	
Gaston	Fantasyland	
Lady Tremaine, Anastasia, Drizella	Fantasyland	

Animal Kingdom Meet n Greets

Character Name	Park Location	Want to Meet ?
Mickey and Minnie (in safari gear)	Adventurers Outpost	
Chip 'n' Dale	DinoLand	
Donald Duck	DinoLand	
Goofy	DinoLand	
Pluto	DinoLand	
Launchpad McQuack	DinoLand	
Scrooge McDuck	DinoLand	
Rafiki and Timon	Character Landing on Discovery Island	
Pocahontas	Discovery Island trail	
Russell and Dug	Discovery Island	

NB: We've tried not to alter our planners too much in the hope that things at Disney will be back to the way they used to be, but some features and attractions may be temporarily suspended in the parks.

Park Character Meet Wish List

Hollywood Studio Meet n Greets
You can find further character dining in the appendix

Character Name	Park Location	Want to Meet ?
Olaf	Echo Lake	
Sorcerer Mickey	Animation Courtyard	
Disney Junior Pals	Animation Courtyard	
Pluto	Animation Courtyard	
Chip 'n' Dale	Sid Cahuenga's One-of-a-Kind	
Mr. and Mrs. Incredible, Edna Mode	Pixar Place	
Buzz Lightyear	Toy Story Land	
Woody and Jessie	Toy Story Land	
BB-8	Launch Bay	
Chewbacca	Launch Bay	
Kylo Ren	Launch Bay	
Rey, Vi Moradi, Chewbacca	Batuu Galaxy's Edge	
Storm Troopers	Batuu Galaxy's Edge	

Epcot Meet n Greets

Character Name	Park Location	Want to Meet ?
Anna and Elsa	Norway Royal Sommerhus	
Joy	ImageWorks	
Donald Duck	Mexico	
Mulan	China	
Princess Aurora	France	
Belle	France	
Alice in Wonderland	United Kingdom	
Snow White	Germany	
Winne the Pooh	United Kingdom	
Vanellope and Ralph	ImageWorks	
Mary Poppins	United Kingdom	

NB: We've tried not to alter our planners too much in the hope that things at Disney will be back to the way they used to be, but some features and attractions may be temporarily suspended in the parks.

Parades and Shows List

List of Parades and Shows we want to see

NB: We've tried not to alter our planners too much in the hope that things at Disney will be back to the way they used to be, but some features and attractions may be temporarily suspended in the parks.

Show Name	Park	Location	Start Time

Park Ride Information

Ride Heights, Genie+ and Individual Lightening Lanes

MINIMUM HEIGHT REQUIREMENTS
FOR EVERY RIDE AT DISNEY'S
MAGIC KINGDOM

ANY HEIGHT

- Astor Orbiter
- Carousel of Progress
- Country Bear Jamboree
- Dumbo the Flying Elephant
- Enchanted Tales with Belle
- Enchanted Tiki Room
- The Hall of Presidents
- Haunted Mansion
- It's A Small World
- Journey of the Little Mermaid
- Jungle Cruise
- Liberty Square Riverboat
- Mad Tea Party
- Magic Carpets of Aladdin W
- innie the Pooh
- Mickey's Philharmagic
- Monsters Inc Laugh Floor
- Peter Pan's Flight
- PeopleMover
- Pirates of the Caribbean
- Prince Charming Carousel
- Space Ranger Spin
- Swiss Family Treehouse
- Tom Sawyer Island
- Walt Disney World Railroad

32 - 38 INCHES

- The Barnstormer - 35"
- Seven Dwarfs Mine Train - 38"
- Tomorrowland Speedway - 32"

40 - 44 INCHES

- Big Thunder Mountain - 40"
- Splash Mountain - 40"
- Space Mountain - 44"

Genie+ Attraction List*

Magic Kingdom
Haunted Mansion
Big Thunder Mountain Railroad
Splash Mountain
Buzz Lightyear's Space Ranger Spin
Monsters, Inc. Laugh Floor
Tomorrowland Speedway
The Many Adventures of Winnie the Pooh
Under the Sea – Journey of the Little Mermaid
Mickey's PhilharMagic
Mad Tea Party
Peter Pan's Flight
"it's a small world"
Pirates of the Caribbean
Jungle Cruise
Dumbo the Flying Elephant
The Barnstormer
The Magic Carpets of Aladdin

Individual Lightening Lane

Ride	Cost $

Notes

_____
_____
_____
_____
_____

*Ride lists are subject to change, please refer to Disneyworld sites for accuracy. Its also our advice to check Individual Lightening Lame Rides nearer to visit date as these are changeable

Park Ride Information

Ride Heights, Genie+ and Individual Lightening Lanes

MINIMUM HEIGHT REQUIREMENTS
FOR EVERY RIDE AT DISNEY'S
HOLLYWOOD STUDIOS

ANY HEIGHT

- Lightning McQueen's Racing Academy
- Muppet Vision 3D
- Star Wars Launch Bay
- Toy Story Mania
- Walt Disney Presents
- Mickey & Minnie's Runaway Railway

32 - 38 INCHES

- Alien Swirling Saucers - 32"
- Millenium Falcon - Smuggler's Run - 38"
- Slinky Dog Dash - 38"

40 - 48 INCHES

- Rockin' Rollercoaster - 48"
- Star Tours - 40"
- Star Wars: Rise of the Resistance - 40"
- Twilight Zone: Tower of Terror - 40"

Genie+ Attraction List*

Hollywood Studios
- Millennium Falcon: Smuggler's Run
- Slinky Dog Dash
- Star Tours
- Tower of Terror
- Rock 'n' Roller Coaster Starring Aerosmith
- Indiana Jones Epic Stunt
- Toy Story Mania
- Alien Swirling Saucers
- Muppet*Vision 3D
- Frozen Sing-Along Celebration
- Beauty and the Beast — Live on Stage
- Disney Junior — Live on Stage

Individual Lightening Lane

Ride	Cost $

Notes

_____
_____
_____
_____
_____

*Ride lists are subject to change, please refer to Disneyworld sites for accuracy. Its also our advice to check Individual Lightening Lame Rides nearer to visit date as these are changeable.

Park Ride Information

Ride Heights, Genie+ and Individual Lightening Lanes

MINIMUM
HEIGHT REQUIREMENTS
FOR EVERY RIDE AT DISNEY'S
ANIMAL KINGDOM

ANY HEIGHT

- Disney Animals
- The Animation Experience
- The Bone Yard
- Conservation Station
- Dino-Sue
- Discovery Island Trails
- Fossil Fun Games
- Gorilla Falls Exploration Trail
- Habitat Habit
- It's Tough To Be A Bug
- Kilimanjaro Safaris
- Maharajah Jungle Trek
- Tree of Life
- Triceratop Spin
- Wilderness Explorers
- Wild Life Express Train

38 - 48 INCHES

- Kali River Rapids - 38"
- Avatar Flight of Passage - 44"
- Dinosaur - 40"
- Expedition Everest - 44"
- Primeval Whirl - 48"

Genie+ Attraction List*

Animal Kingdom
- Kilimanjaro Safaris
- Festival of the Lion King
- Kali River Rapids
- Feathered Friends in Flight!
- DINOSAUR
- It's Tough to Be a Bug
- Na'vi River Journey
- The Animation Experience

Individual Lightening Lane

Ride	Cost $

Notes

_____
_____
_____
_____
_____

*Ride lists are subject to change, please refer to Disneyworld sites for accuracy. Its also our advice to check Individual Lightening Lame Rides nearer to visit date as these are changeable.

Park Ride Information

Ride Heights, Genie+ and Individual Lightening Lanes

MINIMUM HEIGHT REQUIREMENTS
FOR EVERY RIDE AT DISNEY'S
EPCOT

ANY HEIGHT

- Advanced Training Lab
- The American Adventure
- Bruce's Shark World
- Canada Far & Wide
- Disney & Pixar Short Film Festival
- Agent P's World Showcase Adventure
- Frozen Ever After
- Grand Fiesta Tour
- Journey Into Imagination with Figment
- Kidcot Fun Stops
- Living with the Land
- Seas with Nemo and Friends
- Spaceship Earth
- Turtle Talk with Crush
- The Epcot Exerience
- Impressions de France
- Beauty and the Beast Sing Along
- Reflections of China

40 INCHES

- Mission Space - 40"
- Soarin' Around the World - 40"
- Test Track 40"

Genie+ Attraction List*

EPCOT
- Spaceship Earth
- Soarin'
- Living With the Land
- Test Track
- Journey Into Imagination with Figment
- Disney & Pixar Short Film Festival
- Turtle Talk with Crush
- The Seas with Nemo and Friends
- Mission: SPACE

Individual Lightening Lane

Ride	Cost $

Notes

_____
_____
_____
_____
_____

*Ride lists are subject to change, please refer to Disneyworld sites for accuracy. Its also our advice to check Individual Lightening Lame Rides nearer to visit date as these are changeable.

RIDE PLANS & Reservations
Plan your Disney Park Day Reservations

AT PRESENT AND POSSIBLY FOR THE FORESEEABLE FUTURE DISNEY WORLD PARKS WILL REQUIRE YOU TO HAVE BOOKED YOUR INTENDED PARK VISIT IN ADVANCE...

STEP 1 – Ensure you have purchased a park ticket, single days or a 7 or 14 day ultimate ticket and that it is linked to your *My Disney Experience* (MDE) app. Disney packages will show you have a linked park ticket in your MDE app once you have linked your hotel reservation.

STEP 2 – Create your party from your friends and family list.

STEP 3 – Select a date and park that you would like to visit from the available options. You can view the theme park availability online at Disney World's website. (https://www.disneyworld.co.uk/availability-calendar/)

STEP 4 – Review and Confirm our plans and check that the park day shows in your MY PLANS section of your app.

Note: Without prior advanced park bookings you will not be admitted to the park on the day.

RIDE PLANS & Reservations
Plan your Disney Park Day Reservations

DATE	PARK	DATE	PARK
Saturday DATE:		**Saturday** DATE:	
Sunday DATE:		**Sunday** DATE:	
Monday DATE:		**Monday** DATE:	
Tuesday DATE:		**Tuesday** DATE:	
Wednesday DATE:		**Wednesday** DATE:	
Thursday DATE:		**Thursday** DATE:	
Friday DATE:		**Friday** DATE:	

RIDE PLANS & Reservations
Plan your Disney Park Day Reservations

DATE	PARK	DATE	PARK
Saturday DATE:		Saturday DATE:	
Sunday DATE:		Sunday DATE:	
Monday DATE:		Monday DATE:	
Tuesday DATE:		Tuesday DATE:	
Wednesday DATE:		Wednesday DATE:	
Thursday DATE:		Thursday DATE:	
Friday DATE:		Friday DATE:	

RIDE PLANS & Reservations
Genie+ Lightening Lane Fast Pass

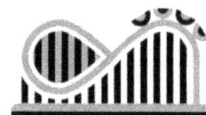

GENIE+ AT DISNEY WORLD

- COSTS $15 PER TICKET, PER DAY. (SUBJECT TO CHANGE)

- GRANTS FASTER ACCESS TO 46 ATTRACTIONS USING THE LIGHTNING LANE ENTRANCE.

- CAN MAKE ONE RESERVATION AT A TIME THROUGHOUT THE DAY.

- ONCE THE INITIAL SELECTION IS REDEEMED OR THE ARRIVAL WINDOW HAS PASSED, GUESTS CAN MAKE ANOTHER SELECTION UP TO PARK CLOSING.

- DOES NOT INCLUDE PHOTOPASS.

- GUESTS CAN MAKE THEIR INITIAL GENIE+ SELECTION BEGINNING AT 7 A.M. ON THE DAY OF THEIR VISIT.

- SELECTIONS CAN BE MADE ACROSS THEME PARKS FOR ELIGIBLE PARK HOPPERS.

- STANDBY LINES REMAIN FREE.

- VIRTUAL QUEUES ARE FREE BUT HAVE A PAID OPTION WITH INDIVIDUAL LIGHTNING LANE SELECTIONS.

- AUDIO EXPERIENCES TAILORED TO SPECIFIC LOCATIONS THROUGHOUT THE LANDS.

RIDE PLANS & Reservations
Genie+ Budget Planner

DATE: DAY: Park Name	Genie+ Cost $	Individual Ride Cost $
		1)
		2)
		3)
Notes:	Total:	Total :
	GRAND TOTAL	$

DATE: DAY: Park Name	Genie+ Cost $	Individual Ride Cost $
		1)
		2)
		3)
Notes:	Total:	Total :
	GRAND TOTAL	$

DATE: DAY: Park Name	Genie+ Cost $	Individual Ride Cost $
		1)
		2)
		3)
Notes:	Total:	Total :
	GRAND TOTAL	$

RIDE PLANS & Reservations
Genie+ Budget Planner

DATE: DAY: Park Name	Genie+ Cost $	Individual Ride Cost $
		1)
		2)
		3)
Notes:	Total:	Total :
	GRAND TOTAL	$

DATE: DAY: Park Name	Genie+ Cost $	Individual Ride Cost $
		1)
		2)
		3)
Notes:	Total:	Total :
	GRAND TOTAL	$

DATE: DAY: Park Name	Genie+ Cost $	Individual Ride Cost $
		1)
		2)
		3)
Notes:	Total:	Total :
	GRAND TOTAL	$

RIDE PLANS & Reservations
Genie+ Budget Planner

DATE: DAY: Park Name	Genie+ Cost $	Individual Ride Cost $
		1)
		2)
		3)
Notes:	Total:	Total :
	GRAND TOTAL	$

DATE: DAY: Park Name	Genie+ Cost $	Individual Ride Cost $
		1)
		2)
		3)
Notes:	Total:	Total :
	GRAND TOTAL	$

DATE: DAY: Park Name	Genie+ Cost $	Individual Ride Cost $
		1)
		2)
		3)
Notes:	Total:	Total :
	GRAND TOTAL	$

RIDE PLANS & Reservations
Genie+ Budget Planner

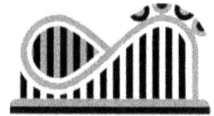

DATE: DAY: Park Name	Genie+ Cost $	Individual Ride Cost $
		1)
		2)
		3)
Notes:	Total:	Total :
	GRAND TOTAL	**$**

DATE: DAY: Park Name	Genie+ Cost $	Individual Ride Cost $
		1)
		2)
		3)
Notes:	Total:	Total :
	GRAND TOTAL	**$**

DATE: DAY: Park Name	Genie+ Cost $	Individual Ride Cost $
		1)
		2)
		3)
Notes:	Total:	Total :
	GRAND TOTAL	**$**

RIDE PLANS & Reservations
Genie+ Budget Planner

DATE: DAY: Park Name	Genie+ Cost $	Individual Ride Cost $
		1)
		2)
		3)
Notes:	Total:	Total :
	GRAND TOTAL	$

DATE: DAY: Park Name	Genie+ Cost $	Individual Ride Cost $
		1)
		2)
		3)
Notes:	Total:	Total :
	GRAND TOTAL	$

DATE: DAY: Park Name	Genie+ Cost $	Individual Ride Cost $
		1)
		2)
		3)
Notes:	Total:	Total :
	GRAND TOTAL	$

Daily Park Planner

DAY: **DATE:**   /   /

Park:

Hours: **EMH:**

ARRIVAL TIME	TRANSPORTATION	DON'T FORGET...

- - - - - - Attraction / Rides - - - - - -

Genie + Today?   YES ☐

Lightening Ride:_____ YES ☐

Lightening Ride:_____ YES ☐

Lightening Ride:_____ YES ☐

- - Character meets / viewing - -

1:

2:

3:

4:

- - - - - - Dining & Meal Plans - - - - - -

B:

L:

D:

S:

- - - - - - Ride Booking - - - - - -

Genie + Booking Opening

Time: [   ] *Disney* Genie+

- - - - - - - To do list - - - - - - -

- *Use Genie App*
-
-
-
-
-
-
-
-
-
-
-

- - - - - - - - - - - Notes -

_____

_____

_____

Daily Park Planner

DAY: **DATE:**   /   /

Park:	
Hours:	**EMH:**

ARRIVAL TIME	TRANSPORTATION	DON'T FORGET...

------- Attraction / Rides -------

Genie + Today?   YES ☐

Lightening Ride:_____ YES ☐

Lightening Ride:_____ YES ☐

Lightening Ride:_____ YES ☐

-- Character meets / viewing --

1:

2:

3:

4:

------ Dining & Meal Plans ------

B:

L:

D:

S:

------- Ride Booking -------

Genie + Booking Opening

Time: [_____]   *Disney* Genie+

-------- To do list -------

- *Use Genie App*
-
-
-
-
-
-
-
-
-
-
-

------------ Notes ------------

_____

_____

_____

Daily Park Planner

DAY: **DATE:**   /   /

Park:	
Hours:	**EMH:**

ARRIVAL TIME	TRANSPORTATION	DON'T FORGET...

- - - - - - Attraction / Rides - - - - - - -

Genie + Today?	YES	☐
Lightening Ride:_____	YES	☐
Lightening Ride:_____	YES	☐
Lightening Ride:_____	YES	☐

- - Character meets / viewing - -

1:
2:
3:
4:

- - - - - - Dining & Meal Plans - - - - - -

B:
L:
D:
S:

- - - - - - - Ride Booking - - - - - - -

Genie + Booking Opening

Time: [   ]   *Disney* Genie+

- - - - - - - - To do list - - - - - - -

- *Use Genie App*
-
-
-
-
-
-
-
-
-
-

- - - - - - - - - - - Notes -

_____

_____

_____

Daily Park Planner

DAY:　　**DATE:**　/　/

Park:

Hours:　　　　　EMH:

ARRIVAL TIME	TRANSPORTATION	DON'T FORGET...

------- Attraction / Rides -------

Genie + Today?　　　　　YES ☐
Lightening Ride:_____ YES ☐
Lightening Ride:_____ YES ☐
Lightening Ride:_____ YES ☐

-- Character meets / viewing --

1:
2:
3:
4:

------ Dining & Meal Plans ------

B:
L:
D:
S:

------- Ride Booking -------

Genie + Booking Opening

Time: [　　　　]　　Disney Genie+

-------- To do list --------

• *Use Genie App*
•
•
•
•
•
•
•
•
•
•

------------- Notes -------------

_____
_____
_____

Daily Park Planner

DAY:　　　　**DATE:**　/　/

Park:	
Hours:	EMH:

ARRIVAL TIME	TRANSPORTATION	DON'T FORGET...

------ **Attraction / Rides** ------

Genie + Today?　　　　　YES ☐
Lightening Ride:_____ YES ☐
Lightening Ride:_____ YES ☐
Lightening Ride:_____ YES ☐

-- **Character meets / viewing** --

1:
2:
3:
4:

------ **Dining & Meal Plans** ------

B:
L:
D:
S:

------- **Ride Booking** -------

Genie + Booking Opening

Time: [＿＿＿＿] Disney Genie+

------- **To do list** -------

- *Use Genie App*
-
-
-
-
-
-
-
-
-
-

------------- **Notes** -------------

_____
_____
_____

Daily Park Planner

DAY: **DATE:**   /   /

| Park: |
| Hours: | EMH: |

ARRIVAL TIME	TRANSPORTATION	DON'T FORGET...

------- Attraction / Rides -------

Genie + Today?   YES ☐
Lightening Ride:_____ YES ☐
Lightening Ride:_____ YES ☐
Lightening Ride:_____ YES ☐

-- Character meets / viewing --

1:
2:
3:
4:

------ Dining & Meal Plans ------

B:
L:
D:
S:

------- Ride Booking -------

Genie + Booking Opening

Time: ☐   *Disney* Genie+

------- To do list -------

- *Use Genie App*
-
-
-
-
-
-
-
-
-
-
-
-

------------ Notes ------------

_____

_____

_____

Daily Park Planner

DAY: **DATE:**   /   /

Park:
Hours: EMH:

ARRIVAL TIME	TRANSPORTATION	DON'T FORGET...

------- Attraction / Rides -------

Genie + Today?   YES ☐

Lightening Ride:_____ YES ☐

Lightening Ride:_____ YES ☐

Lightening Ride:_____ YES ☐

-- Character meets / viewing --

1:

2:

3:

4:

------ Dining & Meal Plans ------

B:

L:

D:

S:

------- Ride Booking -------

Genie + Booking Opening

Time: [   ] *Disney* Genie+

------- To do list -------

- *Use Genie App*
-
-
-
-
-
-
-
-
-
-

------------ Notes ------------

_____

_____

_____

Daily Park Planner

DAY:　　　　**DATE:**　　/　　/

| Park: |
| Hours: | EMH: |

ARRIVAL TIME	**TRANSPORTATION**	**DON'T FORGET...**

------- Attraction / Rides -------

Genie + Today?　　　　　　　YES ☐
Lightening Ride:_____ YES ☐
Lightening Ride:_____ YES ☐
Lightening Ride:_____ YES ☐

-- Character meets / viewing --

1:
2:
3:
4:

------ Dining & Meal Plans ------

B:
L:
D:
S:

------- Ride Booking -------

Genie + Booking Opening

Time: ☐☐☐☐　*Disney* Genie+

-------- To do list --------

- *Use Genie App*
-
-
-
-
-
-
-
-
-
-
-

------------- Notes ------------------------------------

_____

_____

_____

Daily Park Planner

DAY: **DATE:**   /   /

| Park: |
| Hours: EMH: |

ARRIVAL TIME	TRANSPORTATION	DON'T FORGET...

------- Attraction / Rides -------

Genie + Today?   YES ☐
Lightening Ride:_____ YES ☐
Lightening Ride:_____ YES ☐
Lightening Ride:_____ YES ☐

-- Character meets / viewing --

1:
2:
3:
4:

------ Dining & Meal Plans ------

B:
L:
D:
S:

------- Ride Booking -------

Genie + Booking Opening

Time: [   ]   Disney Genie+

-------- To do list -------

- *Use Genie App*
-
-
-
-
-
-
-
-
-
-

-------------- Notes -------------------------------------

_____

_____

_____

Daily Park Planner

DAY: **DATE:**   /   /

Park:
Hours: EMH:

ARRIVAL TIME	TRANSPORTATION	DON'T FORGET...

------- **Attraction / Rides** -------

Genie + Today?   YES ☐
Lightening Ride:_____ YES ☐
Lightening Ride:_____ YES ☐
Lightening Ride:_____ YES ☐

-- **Character meets / viewing** --

1:
2:
3:
4:

------ **Dining & Meal Plans** ------

B:
L:
D:
S:

------- **Ride Booking** -------

Genie + Booking Opening

Time: ☐   *Disney* Genie+

-------- **To do list** --------

- *Use Genie App*
-
-
-
-
-
-
-
-
-
-
-

------------- **Notes** -------------

_____
_____
_____

Daily Park Planner

DAY: **DATE:**   /   /

| Park: |
| Hours: EMH: |

ARRIVAL TIME	TRANSPORTATION	DON'T FORGET...

------ Attraction / Rides ------

Genie + Today?   YES ☐
Lightening Ride:_____ YES ☐
Lightening Ride:_____ YES ☐
Lightening Ride:_____ YES ☐

-- Character meets / viewing --

1:
2:
3:
4:

------ Dining & Meal Plans ------

B:
L:
D:
S:

------ Ride Booking ------

Genie + Booking Opening

Time: ☐   *Disney* Genie+

------ To do list ------

- *Use Genie App*
-
-
-
-
-
-
-
-
-
-

----- Notes -----

_____
_____
_____

Daily Park Planner

DAY:　　　　**DATE:**　/　/

Park:

Hours:　　　　　EMH:

ARRIVAL TIME	TRANSPORTATION	DON'T FORGET...

------- Attraction / Rides -------

Genie + Today?　　　　　YES ☐
Lightening Ride:_____ YES ☐
Lightening Ride:_____ YES ☐
Lightening Ride:_____ YES ☐

-- Character meets / viewing --

1:
2:
3:
4:

------ Dining & Meal Plans ------

B:
L:
D:
S:

------- Ride Booking -------

Genie + Booking Opening

Time: ☐　　　Disney Genie+

------- To do list -------

• *Use Genie App*
•
•
•
•
•
•
•
•
•
•

-------------- Notes --------------

_____
_____
_____

Daily Park Planner

DAY: **DATE:**   /   /

Park:

Hours: EMH:

ARRIVAL TIME	TRANSPORTATION	DON'T FORGET...

------- Attraction / Rides -------

Genie + Today?   YES ☐

Lightening Ride:_____ YES ☐

Lightening Ride:_____ YES ☐

Lightening Ride:_____ YES ☐

-- Character meets / viewing --

1:

2:

3:

4:

------ Dining & Meal Plans ------

B:

L:

D:

S:

------- Ride Booking -------

Genie + Booking Opening

Time: [ ]   *Disney* Genie+

-------- To do list --------

- *Use Genie App*
-
-
-
-
-
-
-
-
-
-

------------- Notes -------------

_____

_____

_____

Daily Park Planner

DAY: **DATE:**   /   /

| Park: |
| Hours: EMH: |

ARRIVAL TIME	TRANSPORTATION	DON'T FORGET...

------- Attraction / Rides -------

Genie + Today?   YES ☐
Lightening Ride:_____ YES ☐
Lightening Ride:_____ YES ☐
Lightening Ride:_____ YES ☐

-- Character meets / viewing --

1:
2:
3:
4:

------ Dining & Meal Plans ------

B:
L:
D:
S:

------- Ride Booking -------

Genie + Booking Opening

Time: ☐   *Disney* Genie+

-------- To do list --------

- *Use Genie App*
-
-
-
-
-
-
-
-
-

------------- Notes -------------------------------

_____

_____

_____

Daily Park Planner

DAY:　　　　**DATE:**　　/　　/

Park:

Hours:　　　　　　　EMH:

ARRIVAL TIME	TRANSPORTATION	DON'T FORGET...

------ Attraction / Rides -------

Genie + Today?　　　　　YES ☐
Lightening Ride:_____ YES ☐
Lightening Ride:_____ YES ☐
Lightening Ride:_____ YES ☐

-- Character meets / viewing --

1:
2:
3:
4:

------ Dining & Meal Plans ------

B:
L:
D:
S:

-------- Ride Booking -------

Genie + Booking Opening

Time: ⬜ *Disney* Genie+

-------- To do list -------

• *Use Genie App*
•
•
•
•
•
•
•
•
•
•
•

-------------- Notes --------------

_____

_____

_____

Daily Park Planner

DAY: **DATE:**   /   /

| Park: |
| Hours: EMH: |

ARRIVAL TIME	TRANSPORTATION	DON'T FORGET...

------- **Attraction / Rides** -------

Genie + Today?   YES ☐
Lightening Ride:_____ YES ☐
Lightening Ride:_____ YES ☐
Lightening Ride:_____ YES ☐

-- **Character meets / viewing** --

1:
2:
3:
4:

------ **Dining & Meal Plans** ------

B:
L:
D:
S:

------- **Ride Booking** -------

Genie + Booking Opening

Time: ☐   *Disney* Genie+

-------- **To do list** -------

• *Use Genie App*
•
•
•
•
•
•
•
•
•
•

------------- **Notes** -------------

_____
_____
_____

Daily Park Planner

DAY: **DATE:**   /   /

| Park: |
| Hours: EMH: |

ARRIVAL TIME	TRANSPORTATION	DON'T FORGET...

------ **Attraction / Rides** ------

Genie + Today?	YES ☐
Lightening Ride:_____	YES ☐
Lightening Ride:_____	YES ☐
Lightening Ride:_____	YES ☐

-- **Character meets / viewing** --

1:
2:
3:
4:

------ **Dining & Meal Plans** ------

B:
L:
D:
S:

------ **Ride Booking** ------

Genie + Booking Opening

Time: [   ] *Disney* **Genie+**

-------- **To do list** --------

- *Use Genie App*
-
-
-
-
-
-
-
-
-
-

------------ **Notes** ------------

_____

_____

_____

Daily Park Planner

DAY: **DATE:** / /

Park:	
Hours:	**EMH:**

ARRIVAL TIME	TRANSPORTATION	DON'T FORGET...

------- Attraction / Rides -------

Genie + Today?	YES	☐
Lightening Ride:_____	YES	☐
Lightening Ride:_____	YES	☐
Lightening Ride:_____	YES	☐

-- Character meets / viewing --

1:
2:
3:
4:

------ Dining & Meal Plans ------

B:
L:
D:
S:

------- Ride Booking -------

Genie + Booking Opening

Time: [   ] *Disney* Genie+

------- To do list -------

- *Use Genie App*
-
-
-
-
-
-
-
-
-
-

------------- Notes -------------

_____

_____

_____

Daily Park Planner

DAY: **DATE:**   /   /

Park:

Hours: EMH:

ARRIVAL TIME	TRANSPORTATION	DON'T FORGET...

------- Attraction / Rides -------

Genie + Today?   YES ☐
Lightening Ride:_____ YES ☐
Lightening Ride:_____ YES ☐
Lightening Ride:_____ YES ☐

-- Character meets / viewing --

1:
2:
3:
4:

------ Dining & Meal Plans ------

B:
L:
D:
S:

------- Ride Booking -------

Genie + Booking Opening

Time: [   ]   *Disney* Genie+

-------- To do list --------

- *Use Genie App*
-
-
-
-
-
-
-
-
-
-

------------- Notes -------------

_____
_____
_____

Daily Park Planner

DAY: **DATE:**   /   /

Park:

Hours: **EMH:**

ARRIVAL TIME	TRANSPORTATION	DON'T FORGET...

------- **Attraction / Rides** -------

Genie + Today?	YES	☐
Lightening Ride:_____	YES	☐
Lightening Ride:_____	YES	☐
Lightening Ride:_____	YES	☐

-- **Character meets / viewing** --

1:
2:
3:
4:

------ **Dining & Meal Plans** ------

B:
L:
D:
S:

------- **Ride Booking** -------

Genie + Booking Opening

Time: ☐   *Disney* Genie+

-------- **To do list** --------

- *Use Genie App*
-
-
-
-
-
-
-
-
-
-

-------------- **Notes** --------------------------------

_____

_____

_____

Non Disney Park Day

Plans:

Location:

ARRIVAL TIME	TRANSPORTATION	DON'T FORGET...

----------- Address -----------

-------- To do list --------

- •
- •
- •
- •
- •
- •
- •
- •
- •
- •
- •
- •
- •
- •

---------- SHOPPING List ---------

------ Dining & Meal plans ------

B:

L:

D:

S:

------------ Notes ------------

_____

_____

_____

Non Disney Park Day

DAY: **DATE:** / /

Plans:

Location:

ARRIVAL TIME	TRANSPORTATION	DON'T FORGET...

------------ Address ------------

-------- To do list --------

-
-
-
-
-
-
-
-
-
-

---------- SHOPPING List ----------

-
-
-
-
-
-
-

------ Dining & Meal plans ------

B:

L:

D:

S:

--------------- Notes ---------------

_____

_____

_____

Non Disney Park Day

DAY: **DATE:**   /   /

Plans:

Location:

ARRIVAL TIME	TRANSPORTATION	DON'T FORGET...

------------ Address -------------

-------- To do list --------

-
-
-
-
-
-
-
-
-
-
-
-

---------- SHOPPING List ---------

------ Dining & Meal plans ------

B:

L:

D:

S:

------------- Notes --

_____

_____

_____

Non Disney Park Day

DAY: **DATE:**   /   /

Plans:

Location:

ARRIVAL TIME	TRANSPORTATION	DON'T FORGET...

------------ Address ------------

---------- SHOPPING List ----------

------ Dining & Meal plans ------

B:

L:

D:

S:

-------- To do list --------

-
-
-
-
-
-
-
-
-
-
-
-
-
-
-

-------------- Notes --------------

_____

_____

_____

Non Disney Park Day

DAY: **DATE:**   /   /

Plans:

Location:

ARRIVAL TIME	TRANSPORTATION	DON'T FORGET...

----------- Address -------------   -------- To do list --------

-
-
-
-
-
----------- SHOPPING List ---------
-
-
-
-
-
------ Dining & Meal plans ------
-
B:
-
L:
-
D:
-
S:
-

-------------- Notes --

_____

_____

_____

Non Disney Park Day

DAY: **DATE:**   /   /

Plans:

Location:

ARRIVAL TIME	TRANSPORTATION	DON'T FORGET…

----------- Address -------------

-------- To do list --------

-
-
-
-
-
-
-
-
-
-
-
-
-
-
-
-

---------- SHOPPING List ---------

------ Dining & Meal plans ------

B:

L:

D:

S:

-------------- Notes -------------------------------

_____

_____

_____

Non Disney Park Day

DAY: **DATE:**   /   /

Plans:

Location:

ARRIVAL TIME	TRANSPORTATION	DON'T FORGET...

------------ Address ------------   -------- To do list --------

-
-
-
-
-
-
-
-
-
-
-
---------- SHOPPING List ---------
-
-
-
-
-

------ Dining & Meal plans ------

B:

L:

D:

S:

------------- Notes ---

_____

_____

_____

Non Disney Park Day

DAY: **DATE:** / /

Plans:

Location:

ARRIVAL TIME	TRANSPORTATION	DON'T FORGET...

------------ Address -------------

-------- To do list --------

-
-
-
-
-
-
-
-
-
-
-
-
-
-
-

--------- SHOPPING List ---------

------ Dining & Meal plans ------

B:

L:

D:

S:

-------------- Notes --------------

_____

_____

_____

Non Disney Park Day

DAY: **DATE:** / /

Plans:

Location:

ARRIVAL TIME	TRANSPORTATION	DON'T FORGET...

----------- Address -----------   -------- To do list --------

-
-
-
-
-
-
-
-
-
----------- SHOPPING List ---------
-
-
-
-
-
------ Dining & Meal plans ------
-
B:
-
L:
-
D:
-
S:

------------ Notes ---------------------------------------

_____

_____

_____

Non Disney Park Day

DAY:　　**DATE:**　　/　　/

Plans:

Location:

ARRIVAL TIME	TRANSPORTATION	DON'T FORGET...

------------ Address ------------

--------- To do list --------

-
-
-
-
-
-
-
-
-
-
-
-
-
-

--------- SHOPPING List ---------

------ Dining & Meal plans ------

B:

L:

D:

S:

------------ Notes --

_____

_____

_____

Souvenir / Gift List

ITEM

□ _____
□ _____
□ _____
□ _____
□ _____
□ _____
□ _____
□ _____
□ _____
□ _____
□ _____
□ _____
□ _____
□ _____
□ _____
□ _____
□ _____
□ _____
□ _____
□ _____
□ _____
□ _____
□ _____
□ _____

ITEM

□ _____
□ _____
□ _____
□ _____
□ _____
□ _____
□ _____
□ _____
□ _____
□ _____
□ _____
□ _____
□ _____
□ _____
□ _____
□ _____
□ _____
□ _____
□ _____
□ _____
□ _____
□ _____
□ _____
□ _____

Souvenir / Gift List

ITEM   ITEM

☐ _____   ☐ _____
☐ _____   ☐ _____
☐ _____   ☐ _____
☐ _____   ☐ _____
☐ _____   ☐ _____
☐ _____   ☐ _____
☐ _____   ☐ _____
☐ _____   ☐ _____
☐ _____   ☐ _____
☐ _____   ☐ _____
☐ _____   ☐ _____
☐ _____   ☐ _____
☐ _____   ☐ _____
☐ _____   ☐ _____
☐ _____   ☐ _____
☐ _____   ☐ _____
☐ _____   ☐ _____
☐ _____   ☐ _____
☐ _____   ☐ _____
☐ _____   ☐ _____
☐ _____   ☐ _____
☐ _____   ☐ _____
☐ _____   ☐ _____
☐ _____   ☐ _____
☐ _____   ☐ _____

Vacation Memoirs

DAY: _____   DATE: /   /

Favourite Part Of The Day:

DAY: _____   DATE: /   /

Favourite Part Of The Day:

Vacation Memoirs

DAY: _____   DATE: ___ / ___ / ___

☆ Favourite Part Of The Day: _____

DAY: _____   DATE: ___ / ___ / ___

☆ Favourite Part Of The Day: _____

Vacation Memoirs

DAY: _____ DATE: __ / __ / __

☆ Favourite Part Of The Day:

DAY: _____ DATE: __ / __ / __

☆ Favourite Part Of The Day:

Vacation Memoirs

DAY: _____ DATE: __ / __ / __

☆ Favourite Part Of The Day:

DAY: _____ DATE: __ / __ / __

☆ Favourite Part Of The Day:

Vacation Memoirs

DAY: _____ DATE: / /

Favourite Part Of The Day:

DAY: _____ DATE: / /

Favourite Part Of The Day:

Vacation Memoirs

DAY: _____ DATE: __ / __ / __
_____
_____
_____
_____
_____
_____
_____
_____

Favourite Part Of The Day:
_____

DAY: _____ DATE: __ / __ / __
_____
_____
_____
_____
_____
_____
_____
_____

Favourite Part Of The Day:
_____

Vacation Memoirs

DAY: _____ DATE: __ / __ / __

\---

\---

\---

\---

\---

\---

\---

\---

Favourite Part Of The Day:

\---

DAY: _____ DATE: __ / __ / __

\---

\---

\---

\---

\---

\---

\---

\---

Favourite Part Of The Day:

\---

Vacation Memoirs

DAY: _____   DATE: /   /

\- \-

\- \-

\- \-

\- \-

\- \-

\- \-

\- \-

Favourite Part Of The Day:

\- \-

DAY: _____   DATE: /   /

\- \-

\- \-

\- \-

\- \-

\- \-

\- \-

\- \-

Favourite Part Of The Day:

\- \-

Vacation Memoirs

DAY: _____ DATE: ___ / ___ / ___

Favourite Part Of The Day:

DAY: _____ DATE: ___ / ___ / ___

Favourite Part Of The Day:

Vacation Memoirs

DAY: _____ DATE: / /
- -
- -
- -
- -
- -
- -
- -
Favourite Part Of The Day:
- -

DAY: _____ DATE: / /
- -
- -
- -
- -
- -
- -
- -
Favourite Part Of The Day:
- -

Vacation Memoirs

DAY: _____ DATE: / /

Favourite Part Of The Day:

DAY: _____ DATE: / /

Favourite Part Of The Day:

Vacation Memoirs

DAY: _____ DATE: __/__/__

⭐ Favourite Part Of The Day:

DAY: _____ DATE: __/__/__

⭐ Favourite Part Of The Day:

Vacation Memoirs

DAY: _____ DATE: __ / __ / __

_____

_____

_____

_____

_____

_____

☆ Favourite Part Of The Day:
_____

DAY: _____ DATE: __ / __ / __

_____

_____

_____

_____

_____

_____

☆ Favourite Part Of The Day:
_____

Vacation Memoirs

DAY: _____   DATE: /   /

⭐ Favourite Part Of The Day:

DAY: _____   DATE: /   /

⭐ Favourite Part Of The Day:

Vacation Memoirs

DAY: _____   DATE: /   /

Favourite Part Of The Day:

DAY: _____   DATE: /   /

Favourite Part Of The Day:

Vacation Memoirs

DAY: DATE: /   /

_____

_____

_____

_____

_____

_____

_____

_____

_____

☆ Favourite Part Of The Day:

_____

DAY: DATE: /   /

_____

_____

_____

_____

_____

_____

_____

_____

_____

☆ Favourite Part Of The Day:

_____

Notes

Notes

Appendix – Restaurant List

MAGIC KINGDOM RESTAURANTS

Snack Stops
- Aloha Isle
- Auntie Gravity's Galactic Goodies
- Cheshire Café
- Cool Ship
- Gaston's Tavern
- Joffrey's Coffee & Tea Company
- Liberty Square Market
- Main Street Bakery
- Plaza Ice Cream Parlor
- Prince Eric's Village Market
- Sleepy Hollow
- Storybook Treats
- Sunshine Tree Terrace
- Westward Ho

Table Service Restaurants & Fine Dining
- Be Our Guest Restaurant
- Jungle Navigation Co. LTD Skipper Canteen
- Liberty Tree Tavern
- The Diamond Horseshoe
- The Plaza Restaurant
- Tony's Town Square Restaurant

Quick Service Restaurants
- Casey's Corner
- Columbia Harbour House
- Cosmic Ray's Starlight Café
- Golden Oak Outpost
- Pecos Bill Tall Tale Inn and Café
- Pinocchio Village House
- The Friar's Nook
- The Lunching Pad
- Tomorrowland Terrace Restaurant
- Tortuga Tavern

Disney Character Dining
- Cinderella's Royal Table
- The Crystal Palace

DISNEY'S HOLLYWOOD STUDIOS

Table Service Restaurants & Signature Dining
- 50's Prime Time Café
- Mama Melrose's Ristorante Italiano
- Sci-Fi Dine-In Theater Restaurant
- The Hollywood Brown Derby

Quick Service Restaurants
- ABC Commissary
- Backlot Express
- Catalina Eddie's
- Docking Bay 7 Food and Cargo
- Dockside Diner
- Fairfax Fare
- PizzeRizzo
- Ronto Roasters
- Rosie's All-American Café
- Woody's Lunch Box

Disney Character Dining
- Hollywood & Vine

Lounges
- BaseLine Tap House
- Oga's Cantina
- The Hollywood Brown Derby Lounge
- Tune-In Lounge

Snack & Drink Stands
- Anaheim Produce
- Epic Eats
- Hollywood Scoops
- Joffrey's Coffee & Tea Company
- Kat Saka's Kettle
- KRNR The Rock Station
- Market
- Milk Stand
- Neighborhood Bakery
- The Trolley Car Café

Appendix – Restaurant List

EPCOT DINING

Table Service Restaurants & Fine Dining
- Biergarten Restaurant
- Chefs de France
- Coral Reef Restaurant
- La Hacienda de San Angel
- Le Cellier Steakhouse
- Monsieur Paul
- Nine Dragons Restaurant
- Restaurant Marrakesh
- Rose & Crown Dining Room
- San Angel Inn Restaurante
- Space 220
- Takumi-Tei
- Teppan Edo
- Tokyo Dining
- Tutto Italia Ristorante
- Via Napoli Ristorante e Pizzeria

Quick Service Restaurants
- Katsura Grill
- La Cantina de San Angel
- La Crêperie de Paris
- Les Halles Boulangerie-Patisserie
- Lotus Blossom Café
- Regal Eagle Smokehouse: Craft Drafts & Barbecue
- Sunshine Seasons
- Tangierine Café
- Yorkshire County Fish Shop

Snack & Drink Stands
- Block & Hans
- Choza de Margarita
- Cool Wash
- Crepes des Chefs de France
- Fife & Drum Tavern
- Funnel Cake
- Gelati
- Joffrey's Coffee & Tea Company
- Joy of Tea
- Kabuki Café
- Kringla Bakeri Og Kafe
- The Land Cart
- L'Artisan des Glaces
- Les Vins des Chefs de France
- Popcorn in Canada
- Refreshment Outpost
- Refreshment Port
- Sommerfest
- Traveler's Café
- UK Beer Cart

Disney Character Dining
- Akershus Royal Banquet Hall
- Garden Grill Restaurant

Lounges
- La Cava del Tequila
- Rose & Crown Pub
- Spice Road Table
- Tutto Gusto Wine Cellar

ANIMAL KINGDOM

Table Service Restaurants
- Rainforest Café at Disney's Animal Kingdom
- Tiffins Restaurant
- Yak & Yeti Restaurant

Quick Service Restaurants
- Flame Tree Barbecue
- Harambe Market
- Kusafiri Coffee Shop & Bakery
- Pizzafari
- Restaurantosaurus
- Satu'li Canteen
- Yak & Yeti Local Food Cafes
- Yak & Yeti Quality Beverages

Disney Character Dining
- Tusker House Restaurant

Lounges
- Dawa Bar
- Nomad Lounge

Snack & Drink Stands
- Anandapur Ice Cream Truck
- Caravan Road
- Creature Comforts
- Dino-Bite Snacks
- Dino Diner
- Drinkwallah
- Eight Spoon Café
- Harambe Fruit Market
- Isle of Java
- Joffrey's Coffee & Tea Company
- Mahindi
- Mr. Kamal's
- Pongu Pongu
- Tamu Tamu Refreshments
- Terra Treats
- The Feeding Ground
- The Smiling Crocodile
- Thirsty River Bar & Trek Snacks
- Trilo-Bites
- Warung Outpost

Appendix – Restaurant List

DISNEY SPRINGS RESTAURANTS

- 4R Cantina Barbacoa Food Truck
- AMC Dine-In Theatre / MacGUFFINS
- Amorette's Patisserie
- AristoCrepes
- BB Wolf's Sausage Co
- Beatrix
- Blaze Fast-Fired Pizza
- Chef Art Smith's Homecomin'
- Chicken Guy!
- City Works Eatery and Pour House
- Cookes of Dublin
- D-Luxe Burger
- Disney Food Trucks
- Dockside Margaritas
- Downtown Snow Company
- Earl of Sandwich
- Enzo's Hideaway Tunnel Bar
- Food Truck - Cookie Dough and Everything Sweet
- Frontera Cocina
- Ghirardelli Soda Fountain
- House of Blues Restaurant and Bar
- Häagen-Dazs at Disney Springs West Side
- Jaleo
- Jock Lindsey's Hangar Bar
- Lava Lounge
- Maria and Enzo's Ristorante
- Morimoto Asia
- Morimoto Street Food
- Paddlefish
- Paradiso 37
- Pepe
- Pizza Ponte
- Planet Hollywood Observatory
- Raglan Road
- Rainforest Cafe at Disney Springs Marketplace
- Splitsville Luxury Lanes
- Sprinkles
- Stargazers Bar
- STK Orlando
- T-REX
- Terralina Crafted Italian
- The Basket at Wine Bar George
- The BOATHOUSE
- The Daily Poutine
- The Edison
- The Polite Pig
- The Smokehouse
- Wetzel's Pretzels
- Wetzel's Pretzels at Disney Springs West Side
- Wine Bar George
- Wolfgang Puck Bar and Grill
- Wolfgang Puck Express at Disney Springs Marketplace
- YeSake

BLIZZARD BEACH DINING
- Arctic Expeditions
- Avalunch
- Cooling Hut
- Frostbite Freddy's Frozen Freshments
- I.C. Expeditions
- Lottawatta Lodge
- Mini Donuts
- Polar Pub
- Warming Hut

TYPHOON LAGOON DINING
- Happy Landings Ice Cream
- Leaning Palms
- Let's Go Slurpin'
- Lowtide Lou's
- Snack Shack
- Typhoon Tilly's

Appendix –
Just Character Dining List

- **1900 Park Fare** - Grand Floridian

- **Akershus Royal Banquet Hall** - EPCOT World Showcase

- **Artist Point** - Wilderness Lodge

- **Cape May Cafe** - Beach Club

- **Chef Mickey's Buffet** - Contemporary

- **Cinderella's Royal Table** - Magic Kingdom

- **Garden Grill** - EPCOT Future World

- **Garden Grove** - Swan

- **Hollywood and Vine** - Hollywood Studios

- **Ohana's Best Friends Breakfast featuring Lilo and Stitch** - Polynesian

- **Perfectly Princess Tea Party** - Grand Floridian

- **The Crystal Palace** - Magic Kingdom

- **Topolino's Terrace** - Riviera Resort

- **Trattoria al Forno** - Boardwalk

- **Tusker House Restaurant** - Animal Kingdom

- **Wonderland Tea Party** - Grand Floridian

- **Be Our Guest** – Opportunity to meet the Beast – No guaranteed – Magic Kingdom

- *NEW for 2022 Crown of Corellia Dining Room*

NB: We've tried not to alter our planners too much in the hope that things at Disney will be back to the way they used to be, but some features and attractions may be temporarily suspended in the parks.

Lightning Source UK Ltd.
Milton Keynes UK
UKHW020654051222
413416UK00010B/588

9 781913 587147